# LIFE AT THE POLES

Rita Santos

# EMPEROR PENGUINS

**Enslow Publishing**
101 W. 23rd Street
Suite 240
New York, NY 10011
USA
enslow.com

# WORDS TO KNOW

**adaptation** A feature or behavior that helps a living thing survive.

**blubber** A type of fat that keeps polar animals warm.

**breeding colony** A group of birds hatching eggs together.

**forage** To search for food.

**incubate** To keep an egg warm until it hatches.

**insulate** To add a layer in order to keep warm.

**krill** Small sea animals that look like shrimp.

**predator** An animal that hunts another animal.

**prey** An animal that is hunted for food.

**territorial** Protecting an area.

# CONTENTS

# MADE FOR THE COLD

The land of Antarctica is mainly a polar desert. It is located at the South Pole and has the world's coldest, driest, and windiest conditions. It is also the only place on Earth where emperor penguins live. Most of the land is covered by sea ice. This frozen sea water swells and shrinks with the seasons.

Emperor penguins have many **adaptations** that allow them to survive in the extreme cold. Their outer feathers are waterproof and scale-like. Their inner feathers are soft and trap air close to their skin. This helps them stay warm.

Emperor penguins have adapted to the cold in other ways as well. Their beaks have small nasal passages that hold in body heat. Their bodies are constantly warming the

Emperor penguins have adapted to the frigid conditions of Antarctica.

## Cold Feet

Emperor penguins sometimes stand on their heels to protect their webbed toes from the ice.

blood that goes to and from their feet. This helps prevent frostbite.

## PENGUIN SUITS

The emperor penguin's body is built to survive the harsh climate. It is the largest penguin in the world, with adults standing 48 inches (122 cm). Unlike many other birds, male and female penguins look the same. They both have the same black and white feathers with yellow ear patches. They have strong claws on their feet. These help them grip the ice as they walk. Many other penguin species hop, but emperor penguins do not.

Penguins do not fly. While most birds use their wings to fly, the emperor penguin's wings are more like flippers. They are stiff and flat to help them swim at up to 7 miles (11 km) per hour. On land, penguins are

Emperor penguins have both black and white feathers and bright yellow ear patches.

Penguins take turn sliding down a hill on their bellies. This is known as tobogganing.

slow. A well-fed penguin has up to 3 inches (7.6 cm) of **blubber** to **insulate** it from the chill of its habitat.

# WHAT'S FOR DINNER?

**E**mperor penguins are very social. They are the only kind of penguin that isn't **territorial**. They live and **forage** for food in groups. Penguins live mainly on a diet of fish like the Antarctic silverfish, squid, and **krill.**

Penguins are very social animals. They live, hunt, and even raise their chicks together.

Their tongues have a sharp point that sticks out and helps to trap fish in their mouths.

## DEEP DIVES

The emperor penguin's body has adapted to freezing ocean temperatures. It can also handle the pressure of deep-sea diving. The birds catch prey as far down as 1,800 feet (550 m), which is close to the ocean floor.

Unlike other birds, emperor penguins' bones are solid. This helps to protect them from being crushed as they dive. Their blood also needs less oxygen at lower depths. This

### Going Deep
The longest penguin dive was 27 minutes long.

keeps the birds from passing out when diving.

## PREDATORS

Emperor penguins are close to the top of the food chain. But dangers still exist. On land, birds like the southern giant petrel and the south polar skua search for penguin chicks.

Emperor penguins in Antarctica dive underwater as they hunt for squid.

The leopard seal is one of the few predators of adult emperor penguins.

Penguin parents will violently defend chicks against attacks. They don't always win.

Orcas and leopard seals are the only **predators** who attack adult penguins. Seals hide under ice shelves where the penguins rest. They wait for them to hop into the water and then attack. Penguins that survive the leap swim under sea ice to sneak up on fish. But as they dive back down, orcas like to sneak up on them!

# HUDDLE UP

**E**mperors are the only penguins that mate during the winter months. In March and April, days get shorter. Adult penguins know that it is time to march toward stable pack

The male and female penguins bow their heads towards one another when they are courting.

ice. They may walk as far as 31 to 75 miles (50 to 120 km) inland.

The penguins choose a mate once they reach their **breeding colony**. Penguins only choose one mate per season. In May or June, the female penguin will lay one egg. It weighs a little over 1 pound (453 grams). The mother uses all her energy creating the egg. She then passes it to the male penguin and rushes to the ocean for food. The male stays behind, holding the egg in a special pouch above his feet. He will **incubate** the egg for 65 to 75 days. Male penguins huddle together for warmth during the long, cold winter.

## LIFE AS A CHICK

The shell of a penguin egg is very thick. It can take two or three days for the chick to fully hatch. The female penguins usually

The male and female penguins take turns feeding and caring for their chick.

## Caring for Chicks

Older chicks stay in "crèches" that are watched by a group of penguins. It's like a penguin day care.

haven't returned by the time the chicks arrive. The males feed the chicks with a form of milk from a gland in their throat. When the females return, they take over. They feed the chicks by spitting up meals they have stored up over the winter. The males return to the sea to feed.

Penguin families spend the first few months of the chick's life in the breeding colony. They wait until the chick's adult feathers are almost fully grown before they

Chicks stay close together in large groups to keep warm.

march to the sea. It takes about two months for the chick to shed its soft brown baby feathers. Chicks that make it to adulthood can live nearly 20 years.

# CHANGING PLANET

Emperor Island is in West Antarctica. It was once home to many emperor penguins. In 2011, scientists found that an entire colony that lived on a small island had disappeared. Every year, penguins return to the breeding colonies where they were born. But that winter, no penguins arrived.

## Twice the Fun

In 2017, twin emperor penguins were hatched in an aquarium in China.

Scientists think that they either died out or moved somewhere else. Why did the birds leave?

## SHRINKING HOME

Emperor penguins have adapted to survive in Earth's harshest climate. But climate change threatens the only place they are

As temperatures rise in the Antarctic, ice melts and the penguins lose more of their home.

Humans must take steps now to ensure the future of emperor penguins.

able to live. Rising sea temperatures are causing the sea ice to melt. In some places, too much sea ice can be a problem as well. It can mean penguin parents have to travel farther to feed their chicks.

## WHAT PEOPLE CAN DO

Melting ice doesn't just mean that penguins have a smaller place to live. It also limits their food supply. Penguins feed on krill. This tiny creature feeds on the algae that grows on sea ice. With less ice, there are fewer krill for the penguins.

People can help penguins survive by cutting down on fishing around penguin colonies. We must also take care of the environment. Certain gases we put in the air cause Earth's temperature to rise. People must work together to save these birds and the other animals who make their homes at the poles.

# ACTIVITY

# ROLES AT THE POLES

Everything in an ecosystem is connected. A food web shows all the ways plants and animals in an ecosystem connect to each other. A simple food web is shown on the next page.

You have just learned about the emperor penguin and how it lives in Antarctica. What else lives there? Read over the list of some of the animals found in Antarctica.

## ANIMALS AND MARINE LIFE OF ANTARCTICA

| | |
|---|---|
| Emperor penguins | Krill |
| Orcas | South polar skua |
| Leopard seals | Southern giant petrel |
| Antarctic silverfish | Squid |

Think about what each animal eats. What does an emperor penguin eat? What eats the emperor penguin? You may need to do some research. Then make a food web like the example shown. Show as many connections as you can.

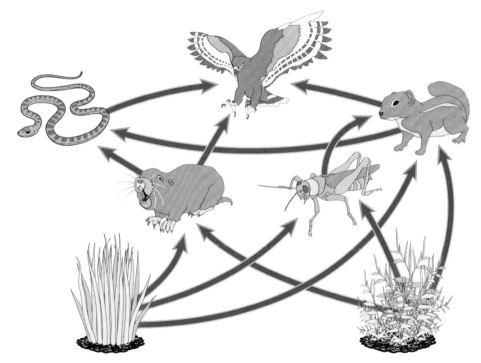

Living things gain energy when they eat. In a food web, arrows point in the direction the energy flows. The grasshopper gets energy from plants and the hawk gets energy from eating the snake.

# Learn More

## BOOKS

Costain, Meredith. *Penguin*. New York, NY: Windmill Books, 2017.

Everett, Reese. *Antarctica*. Vero Beach, Fl.: Rourke Educational Media, 2018.

Waxman, Laura Hamilton. *Emperor Penguins: Antarctic Diving Birds*. Minneapolis, MN: Lerner, 2016.

## WEBSITES

**Active Wild: Antarctica Facts**
*www.activewild.com/antarctica-facts-for-kids/*
Check out pictures, information, and videos about Antarctica.

**National Geographic Kids: Emperor Penguins**
*kids.nationalgeographic.com/animals/emperor-penguin*
Learn more about emperor penguins through games, pictures, and fun facts.

# Index

Published in 2020 by Enslow Publishing, LLC
101 W. 23rd Street, Suite 240, New York, NY 10011

Copyright © 2020 by Enslow Publishing, LLC. All rights reserved.

Library of Congress Cataloging-in-Publication Data

Names: Santos, Rita, author.
Title: Emperor penguins / Rita Santos.
Description: New York : Enslow Publishing, 2020 | Series: Life at the Poles| Audience: Grade K-4. | Includes bibliographical references and index.
Identifiers: LCCN 2019010918| ISBN 9781978512115 (library bound) | ISBN 9781978512092 (paperback) | ISBN 9781978512108 (6 pack)
Subjects: LCSH: Emperor penguin—Juvenile literature.
Classification: LCC QL696.S473 S26 2020 | DDC 598.47—dc23
LC record available at https://lccn.loc.gov/2019010918

Printed in the United States of America

Photos Credits:Emperor Penguins – Research by Bruce Donnola

Cover, p. 1 Mario_Hoppmann/Shutterstock.com; p. 5 Frank Krahmer/Corbis/Getty Images; p. 7 Isabella Pfenninger/Shutterstock.com; p. 8 CG Stocker/Shutterstock.com; p. 9 Simon Bottomley/DigitalVision/Getty Images; p. 11 Bill Curtsinger/National Geographic Image Collection/Getty Images; p. 12 Tarpan/Shutterstock.com; p. 13 Enrique R. Aguirre Aves/Oxford Scientific/Getty Images; p. 15 robert mcgillivray/Shutterstock.com; p. 17 Keren Su/Lonely Planet Images/Getty Images; p. 19 Mlenny/E+/Getty Images; p. 20 Paul Nicklen/National Geographic Image Collection/Getty Images; p. 23 Emre Terim/Shutterstock.com; cover and interior pages (frost pattern) polygraphus/Shutterstock.com